REDNECKIN'
MADE EASY

REDNECKIN'
MADE EASY

BO WHALEY

Rutledge Hill Press
NASHVILLE, TENNESSEE 37210

Material in *Redneckin' Made Easy* first appeared in
The Official Redneck Handbook © 1987
by Bo Whaley and published by Rutledge Hill Press.

Published in Nashville, Tennessee, by Rutledge Hill
Press, Inc., 513 Third Avenue South, Nashville,
Tennessee 37210

Library of Congress Cataloging-in-Publication Data

Whaley, Bo., 1926-
    Redneckin' made easy.

    Excerpts from: The official redneck handbook.
    1. Working class whites—Southern States—Humor.
2. Southern States—Social life and customs—Humor.
I. Title.
PN6231.S64W4325   1988   305.5'63'0207   88-18348
ISBN 0-934395-94-2

2   3   4   5   6   7   8   9—94   93   92   91   90
Manufactured in the United States of America

CONTENTS

INTRODUCTION

The migration of Yankees to the South is at an all-time high these days. This should not surprise us when we pause to consider the prophetic words of that great son of the South, Col. Beauregard P. Hornsby, who said, "I say, son . . . now you ain't never heard of nobody retirin' to th' Nawth, have you?"

REDNECKIN' MADE EASY will prove invaluable to the thundering herds moving to the South daily. It will help them understand their new home. It also will be useful to born rednecks, helping them keep up their self-image and serving as a guide to prevent their falling prey to the Yankee way of doin' things. This little book will have served a valuable purpose if it protects just one good ole boy from bein' corrupted.

Some people are born rednecks ("they have natural talent"), but others have to work hard at it. This book is for both kinds. For those forced to work hard at it, REDNECKIN' MADE EASY is a "how to" book. Once the knack of being a redneck has been mastered, those unfortunate souls remaining above the You'se Guys-Y'all Line (also known as the Mason-Dixon Line) shoveling snow and fighting traffic will envy their counterpoints no end.

Many an aspiring youngster has said, "When I grow up, I want to be a redneck." This book will provide invaluable assistance in helping them get there, and without making any wrong turns. They deserve no less.

Thus REDNECKIN' MADE EASY serves two purposes: to assist Yankees bent on retiring South so they will be better prepared to accept and cope with the life and to point out to those of us who already live here the many blessings we enjoy.

After reading this handbook, anybody will be able to cope anywhere in the South, no matter where he or she was born and raised. So let's get on with it. As the saying goes way down in grits country, "Let's let it all hang out!"

REDNECKIN'
MADE EASY

THE OFFICIAL REDNECK
APTITUDE TEST

Self-appointed experts from the deep South and the far North keep trying to identify and classify the redneck. Some of them know what they're talking about, and some don't.

To aid them in their efforts I have designed what I believe is a foolproof aptitude test for the purpose of determining an individual's redneck traits or tendencies. You would do well to take the test. Better still, take it with a friend who is convinced he's a bigger redneck than you are. Make a friendly wager. Let the loser pay for the long-neck Buds.

REDNECK APTITUDE TEST

	Me	You

1. You get five points if you chew tobacco. Add two more if you dip snuff. You get an additional fifteen points if your grandmother dips snuff. Double that if you've ever kissed a woman who had snuff in her mouth at the time.

2. You get five points if you go swimming in cut-off Levis. If you are female and you wear cut-off Levis and a T-shirt swimming, you get double points. Both male and female subtract ten points if you do your swimming in a swimming pool. But add five points if your dog goes in swimming with you.

3. If you own a polyester leisure suit, give yourself five points. Add five more if you still wear it. Add three more points if you got it from your daddy. Double that if it has any embroidery on it.

4. Give yourself three points if your belt has your name on the back. Add one point for each inch wide the buckle is. Add five points if you carry a knife in a case on the belt. You get five bonus points if you wear a white belt. If you wear white shoes to match the belt, add ten points. And if you wear white socks, add fifteen points.

5. Give yourself five points if you wear cowboy boots. Double it if you sleep in them. Triple it if the boots are made of snake or lizard skin. Subtract fifteen points if they're made in Taiwan or in Massachusetts. Add ten points if you own a horse.

6. You get ten points if you live in a mobile home. Add five more if it's a single-wide. Add two more for every dog that sleeps under it and one point for every tire that's rotted out. Add three for every sliding closet door that works but subtract three points if it's skirted, unless the skirting is rusted tin roofing or cardboard. Add one point for every dish in the sink that needs washing, but subtract a point for every pair of clean socks in the trailer.

7. Give yourself ten points for every car in the yard that's up on cement blocks. Subtract two points for each cement block that you bought. Add one point for each year if it's older than a 1972 model. Subtract five points if it has a battery. Subtract ten points if it's a European sports car. Add ten if you painted it yourself with a brush. Add five if you had it painted by Earl Shieb.

____	____
____	____
____	____
____	____
____	____

8. Score ten points for yourself if you can whistle through your teeth. Add five more if your wife can.

____	____
____	____

9. Give yourself two points for every rifle you own, and add one point for each one with a scope. And give yourself five points if you carry a pistol in the glove compartment of your vehicle. Double that if your wife carries one, too. Triple it if she knows how to use it. Subtract ten points if either of you has a permit.

____	____
____	____
____	____
____	____

10. You get five points if you drive a pickup truck. Add five more if it's a four-wheel drive. Add five more if it has over-sized tires with raised white letters. Add another five if there's a dog box in the back, but subtract ten if the dog is registered. Add one point for every beer can in the back, add one point for each can that is hand-crushed. Subtract three points if the cooler is clean.

____	____
____	____
____	____
____	____
____	____
____	____
____	____
____	____

11. Give yourself four points if you smoke non-menthol cigarettes; and add five more if you smoke non-filter Camels. Subtract five if you don't smoke cigarettes. Add five points if you use stick matches, and two more if you can strike them with your thumbnail or on the seat of your britches. Add another for every hour you keep one in your mouth.

____	____
____	____
____	____
____	____
____	____
____	____

12. Give yourself five points if you've got a boat parked in the yard. Add three if it's a bass boat but subtract three if there are no dead worms in the bottom. Subtract five points if the motor cranks on the first pull. Subtract fifteen if it's a sailboat.

13. Give yourself five points if you have a beard, but subtract three if you bathed yesterday. Add three if all the plumbing works and all your utilities are paid and current.

17

14. You get five points if you wear a white shirt with the sleeves rolled up. Add five more if the shirttail is out. Subtract one point if it only has one pocket, but add a point for each missing button. You must subtract two points if the collar button has ever been buttoned.

15. You get five points if you dropped out of high school. Double that if you were kicked out for fighting. Triple it if you attended for twelve years but failed to graduate.

16. Give yourself twenty points if you listen to country music. Add ten more if you've ever been to Nashville, and ten more if you went to the Grand Ole Opry. Subtract ten if you attended but didn't yell.

18

You lose five more if you don't know where Johnny Cash and Merle Haggard served time. But add five if you can find WSM on your radio.

17. You lose ten points if you know who Pat Benatar is. And you lose twenty if you've ever listened to a whole song by Pat Benatar without changing to another station. You're out of the game and lose by forfeit if you own a Pat Benatar album or tape. But you can be considered for a future game if you can name all four members of the Alabama band.

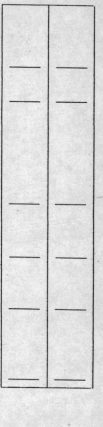

Well, how did you make out? If you feel that you scored high enough to seriously consider making the move South, then you need to keep reading for some helpful hints before making a final decision.

CUT HERE

SPEAKIN' REDNECK
MADE EASY

Don't think for a minute that you can just up and move to redneck country and know what's goin' on right from the very start. Not so. Therefore, it is strongly suggested that you burn the ol' midnight oil in an attempt to memorize as many redneck words and phrases as possible before making the move. Otherwise, you will be just as lost as a redneck in China. You probably wouldn't understand a thing that's said.

There are certain key words that you'll need to know, words that come as natural as rain to a redneck. Having these words at your disposal will greatly ease the transformation.

The words selected have the same meaning north of the Mason-Dixon Line as they do south of it; the only real difference lies in their pronunciation.

By the way, no attempt is being made here to list the words in alphabetical order because it really don't make no difference as I see it. After all, we don't talk in alphabetical order, right?

The redneck spelling of the word is followed by the correct spelling of the word in parentheses. I figure you'll know that, but I ain't takin' no chances. Then there will be an example of how the word can be used in a sentence.

It is also suggested that this section of the book be clipped and saved because you never know when it might come in handy in your new surroundings.

NEVER LEAVE HOME WITHOUT IT!

Word	How It's Used
Kreck (*Correct*):	The kreck spellin' of kreck is "Correct." Lak "My mommer is a skool teecher and tonite she has to kreck tes' papuhs."
Fem (*Film*):	"My an' Buster went to the' maountins an' I tuk my camra, but I'll be dadgummed if'n I did'n f'rgit to buy some fem."

Fem

Doc (*Dark*):	"I'm 19 yeers ol' but I steel sleep with a lite on 'cause I'm skeert o' th' doc."
Idnit (*Isn't it*):	"It shore is purty out t'nite with th' full moon an' all, idnit?"

23

Word	How It's Used
Hard (Hired):	"My Daddy went to th' unemployment offis this mornin' to see 'bout gittin' a job at the new factry whut's openin' nex' month, but for some reason he wan't hard."
Idy (Idea):	"I heered whut ya' sed at th' PTA meetin' las' nite 'bout sponsorin' a chittlin' suppah to raise money f'r th' ban uniforms, Charlotte, an' I thank thas a reel gud idy."
Jevver (Did you ever):	"Bobby Joe tol' me ya' wuz daown at th' Chivverlay place lookin' at one o' them new Impallers. Jevver trade?"
Keer (Care):	"Granny ain't gittin' 'long so good, what with her a' havin' roomytisem an' all. But she's a' doin' bettah since she got on a program called Home Hailth Keer whur nurses come t' visit her to home onc't a week."

Word	How It's Used
Mere *(Mirror):*	"We bin doin' th' crazies' thangs lately in Play Skool, Mary Frances. That new teecher has got us mem'rizin silly verses. Yistitty we had t' larn one whut goes, "Mere, mere, on th' wahl, who's th' faires' uv them awl'. Now then, I ast ya, ain't thet plum' silly?"
Wail *(Well):*	"I jis come fum th' doctor. I ain't rilly bin wail fer a while but wuz too busy to go an' find out whut wuz wrong. Found out I got shootin' pains, whatever th' heck that is."

Mere

Word	How It's Used
Argy *(Argue)*:	"I ain't a' goin' to Lucy Mae's no more. She thanks she knows ever'thang an' she don't know nuthin' a tall. 'Sides, ever time I go to her haouse, all we ivver do is argy."
Bub *(Bulb)*:	"Johnnie Faye! Run daoun to Mr. Johnson's stow an' git me a lite bub—hunnert watt."
Earl *(Aerial)*:	"Josh, we plum' got to buy us a new earl fer th' radio. It's done got to th' pint whur I can't even git WSM an' they ain't no way I ain't gonna' lissen to th' Gran' Ole Opry come Sat'dy nite."
Far *(Fire)*:	"Bobby Joe, go git some stovewood an' bild a far in th' farplace in th' livin' room. Granny's a' comin' this afternoon an' you know how she hates col' weather."
Cocoler *(Coca-Cola)*:	"I want two hamburgers all the way, a awder o' Franch fries an' a Cocoler."

Word	How It's Used
Hep *(Help)*:	"Tell ya' whut I'll do, Lunce. If'n you'll hep me dig my 'taters, I'll hep you cut yore hay."
Awduh *(Order)*:	"I'm gonna' awduh me two dresses an' a hat fum Sears. An' I'm gonna' awduh two pair of ovalls fer Jayssie."

Argy

Wudnit *(Wasn't it)*:	"Boy! Thet shore wuz some scary movie on th' TV las' nite, wudnit?"
All *(Oil)*:	"Lemme hav five dollars wuth o' reg'lar an' a quat o' all, Goober. Ever'thin' ailse is awright."

Word	How It's Used
Bard *(Borrowed):*	"Lucy, I ain't loanin' Buster Bland nothin' ailse. He bard my shovel an' didn't brang hit bak. An' he bard my battry charger an' lost hit."
Bleeve *(Believe):*	"Wail, I kin tail ya' one thang 'baout ol' man Jenkins. Ya' jus' can't bleeve a word he says. I wouldn't bleeve 'im if he wuz a' dyin' an' knowed it."
Kumpny *(Company):*	"Git in heah an' blow yo nose an' warsh yore face, young'un! Don't ya' know we got kumpny a' comin t'nite?"
Gull *(Girl):*	"Who wuz zat gull I seen ya' with las' nite, Bobby Jack? Man! She wuz a hum-dinger!"
Orta *(Ought to):*	"I know dang wail I orta' go ahead an' git my new car tag, but I jus' can't never thank uv it when I'm in taoun."
Nome *(No m'am):*	"Robert! Is ya' did yor Ainglish homework yit?"

"Nome." "Wail, git on hit this minit! Fus' thang ya' know you'll be growed up an' won't have no idy haow t' write 'er tawk a tall."

Rench *(Rinse):* "I used to hav' a bunch o' troubl' with bad breath, m'sef. But I bought me some o' that stuff I seen on the TV whut ya' rench aout ya' mouth with an' I ain't had no more troubl'."

Yale *(Yell):* "Wail naow, Bessie Faye, ya' can't be no cheerleader if'n ya' ain't willin' t' yale. Shoot! You can yale with the bes' uv 'em, so git on aout there an' yale."

29

Word	How It's Used
Umurkin (*American*):	"Did'ja see that feller on th' lebbum o' clock news las' nite burnin' that Umurkin flag up in New Yawk? Sumbody orta' raound him up an' teech 'im a lesson with a tar arn or sum'thin. I don't bleeve he's no Umurkin, nohow."
Tarred (*Tired*):	"Why 'ont y'all go on to th' pitcher show, Zeke. I bin arnin' awl day an' I'm tarred aout."
Treckly (*Later*):	"Y'all go on home an' feed the cows an' slop th' hawgs, Lena. I'll be comin' on treckly."
Whirr (*Where*):	"Whirr you bin, boy? Suppah's bin redy f'r mor'n two ouers."
Ovalls (*Overalls*):	"Somebody answer that tellyphone, an' tell whoever 'tis I'll be there soon's I hang these ovalls on th' line."
Smore (*Some more*):	"Ma, kin I hav smore greeuts?"

Umurkin

Spear *(Superior):* "Daddy said Buddy got coat-marshulled 'cuz he cuassed his spear oficer."

Rernt *(Ruined):* "Know that new coat I bought at th' sale las' week? Well, Harvey spil't battry acid on it an' rernt it."

Prolly *(Probably):* "I ain't reel shore whut we gonna' do this Crismus. We'll prolly go to Mama's."

Summers *(Some-where):* "I 'ont know zackly whirr Chicargo's at, but I believe hit's summers up north close to Illernoise."

Arn *(Iron):* "I tell ya', Hoss, thet ol' boy's tough as pig arn."

Word	How It's Used
Aig (Egg):	"Yeah, I bin t' Savanner twice't. An both times I went thet papuh meal smelt lak a rotten aig."
Plike (Play like):	"Tell ya' whut, Billy Frank; you plike you Tonto and I'll plike I'm th' Lone Ranger."
Ahmoan (I'm going to):	"Ahmoan ast Ma if I kin spen' th' nite at yore house."
Fur (Far):	"How fur is it fum Atlanter to Chattnooger?"
Munt (Month):	"Febererry is th' shortes' munt uf th' yeer."
Moanin (Morning):	"Good moanin', Mr. Weeulson."
Hail (Hell):	"Wail, I'll jus' tail ya' haow I feel 'bout it. If'n she don't lak th' way I dress, she can jus' go straight to hail."
Airs (Errors):	"Anybody whut plays baseball is baound to make airs 'cause they ain't nobody purrfect."
Bay-ed (Bed):	"I feel this way 'baout it. He made his bay-ed, so let 'im sleep in hit."

32

Hail

Lecktristy *(Electricity)*:	"I thank it wuz a feller name of Benjamin Franklin whut faound aout 'bout lecktristy when his Daddy los' patience with him an' tol' him to go fly a kite jus' to git Ben aout o' the haouse."
Cheer *(Chair)*:	"Jus' hang yore coat on the bak o' thet cheer."
Moanbak *(Come on back)*:	"Cut th' stirrin' wheel to th' rite an' moanbak."
Dayum *(Damn)*:	"Frankly, mah deah, I don't giv' a dayum!"
Greeuts *(Grits)*:	"Pleez pass th' greeuts."
Saar *(Sour)*:	"Ma, this meeulk tastes lak hit's saar."
Stow *(Store)*:	"Ah'm goin' to th' stow an' git sum 'baccer. Be rat bak."

33

Word	How It's Used
Spec *(Expect)*:	"I rilly wud lak to stay fer supper, but I spec I bes' be gittin' on home."
Sinner *(Center)*:	"Ol' Charley won th' turkey shoot this mornin'. He flat hit thayet bull's eye dade sinner."
Zat *(Is that)*:	"This here's my cap. Zat yores?"
War *(Wire)*:	"I cud fix this thang in nothin' flat if'n I had me a piece o' war."
Zackly *(Exactly)*:	"Frum Atlanter to Bumminham is zackly 158 miles."
Tawk *(Talk)*:	"Yeah, I watch TV. But I don't watch none o' them tawk shows."
Sawt *(Salt)*:	"This here taoun is gonna' miss ol' man Hipple. He was the sawt o' th' earth."
Pitcher *(Picture)*:	"All right, you young'uns git in th' haouse an' git cleaned up some. We got to go to taoun an' git our pitcher took fer Chrismus."

Word	How It's Used
Ose (Oldsmobile):	"Did'ja heer that Frankie Bennett traded cars las' week? Traded his '72 Ponyack fer a '79 Ose 88."
Ovair (Over there):	"I 'prechate th' offer uv a ride but I kin walk. I ain't goin' fur, jus' rite ovair."

War

Plane, or Balin'

Lectric

Bob

Word	How It's Used
Phrasin (Freezing):	"Somebody put some more wood on th' far. It's phrasin' cold in heer."
Shurf (Sheriff):	"If'n thayet pickup comes by heer jus' one more time a' speedin' I'm gonna' call th' shurf an' hav' 'im locked up."

Word	How It's Used
Madge (*Marriage*):	"Says rat cheer in th' local papuh thayet Ralph Swilley has done ast Mollie Bentley fer her han' in madge."
Abode (*A board*):	"I promised the young'uns I wuz gonna' make um a see-saw, but fus I got to see if'n I kin fin' abode."
Tenshun (*Attention*):	"All right, class. I want all uv y'all to set up an' pay tenshun."
Venchly (*Eventually*):	"Naow then, don't git all upset 'cause we done los' owah fus' 16 ball games. Jus' wuk hard an' don' giv up 'cause we gonna' win a game venchly."
Spishuss (*Suspicious*):	"I wudn't git too close to thayet new boy daown th' road if'n I wuz y'all. I bin a' watchin 'im an' he looks spishuss to me."
Skace (*Scarce*):	"Wail, Lem, looks lak th' pecan crop is gonna' come up short this yeer. Yessir, pecans is gonna' be skace as hen's teeth."

36

Spishuss

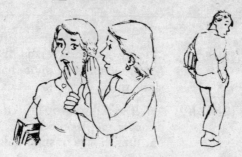

Po *(Poor):*

"Shoot, Roger, you don' know whut bein' po is. They's a fambly ovah in Cedar Creek whut's so po that ever' time they thow a bone out th' bak door th' dog signals fer a fair ketch."

Shaller *(Shallow):*

"Yeah, I guess you young'uns kin go in swimmin'—but be shore ya' stay in th' shaller end."

Cutcha *(Cut you):*

"One thang 'baout ol' Ben, if'n he gits drunk an' mad at th' same time he'll flat cut-cha."

Hesh *(Hush):*

"Hesh yo' maouth, boy! Jes' hesh up!"

Mamanem *(Mama and them):*

"Howdy, Luke. How's yore mamanem?"

Word	How It's Used
Quair *(Queer)*:	"I've always sorta' laked ol' Mr. Woods, but he shore has some quair ways, don't he?"
Shivry *(Chivalry)*:	"Well, thanks fer openin' th' door fer me, Jake. See chillun, th' age o' shivry ain't daid."
Cawk *(Cork)*:	"Anybody know whut happened to th' cawk stopper whut I had in this syrup bottle?"
Cad *(Carried)*:	"I cad some peas ovah to Mrs. Nelson lak ya' tol' me to, Pa. She sed thank you."
Skeert *(Scared)*:	"I'll go fus'. I ain't skeert."
Salary *(Celery)*:	"Tossed salad jus' ain't tossed salad if'n it don't hav sum salary in it."
Less *(Let's)*:	"Less go to th' ball game an' then go git a Big Mac."
Loud *(Allowed)*:	"Mama said we wuzn't loud to go to taoun atter dark."
Foe *(Four)*:	"I ain't memrized it all yet, but I know how it starts off . . . 'Foe sco an' sebum years ago' . . . ."

Shivry

Fussed *(First):*

"Yes, m'am, I know th' answer! Th' fussed man whut walked on th' moon wuz Neil Armstrong."

Doe *(Door):*

"Somebody open th' doe! I got a armload o' stovewood."

Astor *(Ask her):*

"I rilly don' thank Ma's gonna' lemmee go, but I'll astor."

Menshun *(Mention):*

"When ya' git to th' front doe, jus' menshun mah name an' you'll git a good seat."

Nudder *(Another):*

"Mama, kin I hav nudder piece o'cake?"

Leckshun *(election):*

"Can't buy no likker today, Henry. It's leckshun day. Can't nobody but th' politicians git drunk."

Word	How It's Used
Pleese *(Police):*	"Mus' be havin' trouble daoun at th' juke joint. I seen two pleece cars go by."
Lane *(Laying):*	"I ain't worked none since I got laid off in Janawerry, but I'm goin' to wuk nex' week fer a haouse bilder lane tile."
Yistitty *(Yesterday):*	"I gotta' go bak to DEE-troit in the' mornin'. I come in on th' bus late yistitty evenin'."
Rail *(Real):*	"I seen Mr. Sullivan daoun at th' pig sale this mornin' an' I thot he looked rail good."
Blong *(Belong):*	"I don't wanna' go to Sally Mae's birthday party. I jus' don't feel lak I blong there."
Paytrotick *(Patriotic):*	"One o' th' thangs I like bes' 'baout the Foth of July prade is the paytrotick music them bans play."
Sammitch *(Sandwich):*	"No, thank ya' m'am, I done et. Mama fixed me a bloney an' 'mater sammitch."
Tar *(Tire):*	"Weeda' bin here 'fore naow but we had a flat tar jus' aoutside o' Waycross."

Tar

Wangs *(Wings):* "Oh yeah? Well, if'n a frog had wangs he wudn't keep a' bumpin his tail on th' groun."

Ax *(Ask):* "Jus' set there, Ned, an' don't ax so many questions."

Bail *(Bell):* "We bettuh hurry up. I thank I jes' heered th' skool bail rang."

Ball *(Boil):* "Can she cook? Heck, thet ol' gal cudn't ball watah 'thout scorchin' it."

Cane Chew *(Can't you):* "Cane chew jus' see ol' Bobby Jack all decked aout in one o' them monkey suits fer his sister's weddin'?"

41

Word	How It's Used
Legible *(Eligible)*:	"Ain't no way Booger Creek kin win thet football game t'nite 'cause the qwatahbak ain't legible. He flunked Ainglish an' Hist'ry."
Coat *(Court)*:	"I guess we won't be a' seein' much of ol' Jay Bridges fer the nex' few yeers. He got sentenced to eight yeers in Circus Coat this mornin'."
Empire *(Umpire)*:	"Them Atlanter Braves shore got th' shawt end o' the stick agin' them Chicargo Cubs yistitty, did'n they? That fus' base empire flat missed thet play on Murphy at fus base. He wuz safe by two steps."
Tuck *(Took)*:	"I ain't never tuck a drink o' likker in muh life."
Thow *(Throw)*:	"Thayet uppity ol' Hortense Edwards jus' makes me want to thow up."

So much for the vocabulary. There are a couple of other tricks of the redneck trade that, if mastered, will prove invaluable to you in communicating with your new neighbors. These are cardinal rules of redneck grammar and musts for proper Redneck speech:

- Never pronounce the "g" in words endin' with "ing."
- No matter if you're talkin' baout man, woman, child, a haoun' dog, or a pickup truck, put "ol" in front.
- Always put the accent or emphasis on the first syllable of words with two or more. For instance: DEE-troit, UM-breller; IN-shorance; and JU-ly.

And just as a bonus, here's a great redneck line for you to store in your memory bank for future use. It is sure to melt a redneck girlfriend's heart:

"You jus' 'member this, Sugah, Long's I got a biscuit, you got half."

Sorta' chokes a feller up, don't it?

THE DO'S AND DON'TS
OF REDNECKIN'

It should be fully understood by pre-tenders to the world of redneckin' that redneckin' ain't no fad, no passing fancy or a part-time thing. No, sir! Redneckin' is a way of life, either inherited or acquired.

Certain things brand one a Redneck as surely as a forearm tattoo. Therefore, this section is intended to enlighten the uninitiated and never exposed—Yankees—to the wonderful world of redneckin'. The joy of it awaits those willing to do their homework.

Now then, here are some (but by no means all) of the "Do's and Don'ts of Redneckin':

Do

● Say "Yes, m'am" and "No, m'am" and "Yes, sir" and "No, sir" to your mama and daddy.

● Get up before daylight even if you have nowhere to go or nothing to do.

● Always carry a pocket knife. Sharpen it periodically on the sole of your shoe.

● Give all your children nicknames.

● Hang out at gas stations and pool rooms a lot.

● Spend at least two hours a day playing video games.

● Eat lots of boiled peanuts.

● Learn to peel and eat (chew) sugar cane.

● Mash your blackheads in public.

● Get a dog, any dog. Teach him to follow you wherever you go, and to wait for you outside gas stations and pool rooms.

● Call all females, except your mama, "gals."

● Read all the literature you can get your hands on about Robert E. Lee. Hang his picture in your living room.

- Learn to tell the difference right off between a possum and a coon.
- Keep your pickup radio tuned to a country music station.
- Pour your coffee in your saucer and leave the spoon in your iced tea glass.
- Practice the art of crushing beer cans with one hand.

- Pay your child support on time.
- Get a motorcycle from somewhere, preferably a Harley Davidson. Park it in front of a juke joint at least once a week. Sit on it and clean your fingernails with a knife. Spit a lot.
- Hang a pair of fuzzy dice and/or a fish stringer from the rear view mirror of your pickup.

• ALWAYS stand when "Dixie" is played. And let out a rebel yell, "Yaaaaaaaahhhaaaaaaaoooooooeeeee!!" when it is finished.

• Wear long-sleeve shirts, and roll the sleeves up as far as you can—even in winter.

• Cash your paycheck at the nearest 7–11 store.

• Get in the habit of saying things like, "Ya' better bleeve it," "Ya' got that right," and "I ain't lyin', Hoss."

• Go to lots of high school basketball games, and cuss the referees out repeatedly.

- Learn to back an 18-wheeler. And don't forget to kick the tires once in a while.
- Go fishing at least once a week.
- Never work on the opening day of deer or dove season.
- Make regular trips to the wrestling matches, and yell out some of the same things there that you yell out at high school basketball games.
- Try and make an annual trip to Nashville. Spend some time while there on Broadway between Second and Fifth Avenues. Have three or four beers at Tootsie's Orchid Lounge and buy a western outfit or two at The Tony Alamo of Nashville. That will give you instant credibility anywhere in the south. Go to Opryland.
- If you happen to be in South Carolina, buy a big supply of fireworks and smuggle them back home. The young'uns will love it on the Fourth of July and during Christmas. Incidentally, so will the local police.
- Get a bumper sticker that says, "I Seen Rock City."
- Learn to sop syrup.
- Practice until you can make your eggs, grits, ham and biscuits come out even.
- Always eat your steak well done and

your eggs fried hard.

- Display a large Confederate Flag prominently either inside or outside your house, or both.
- Have some knowledge of Herman Talmadge, George Wallace, Lester Maddox and J. B. Stoner.
- Applaud at parades when the United States and Confederate Flags pass. The degree of applause for each is strictly up to you.
- In summer, just peel off your clothes and jump in a river or creek.
- If there is a choice to be made between cutting the grass and going fishing, stand up for your rights as a redneck. And if you catch any, invite your friends to your house for a fish fry. And tell your "old lady" to make up some hushpuppies if she gets through cutting the grass in time.

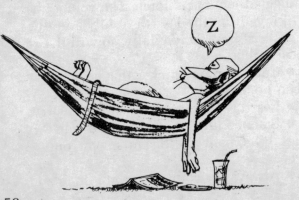

Don't

● Wear sunglasses inside during the daytime.

● Have nothing whatsoever to do with nobody wearing an earring.

● Wear your wrist watch with the face of the watch on the inside of your wrist.

● Wear a pinkie ring.

● Wear your belt with the buckle pointed toward first or third base. Aim it straight for the pitcher's mound.

● Keep your wallet in your front pants pocket.

● Read your horoscope or "Dear Abby." The sports page is where it's at, Hoss.

● Drink hot tea or iced coffee. These are unpardonable sins.

● Watch "The Donahue Show."

● Remove your hat when eatin' with some ol' gal.

● Order potatoes instead of grits. This is just as bad as drinking hot tea or iced coffee.

- Wear anything chartreuse or lavender.
- Get too close to any man who comes from anywhere north of Nashville.
- Button your top shirt button.
- Even own a tie.
- Forget your mama or daddy's birthday.

- Ever talk about how nice *anything* is in New Jersey or New York.
- Have nothin' to do with any sports car.
- Eat no meat that ain't fried.
- Eat in no cafe that serves foreign food.

- Leave home to go on any trip of more than 25 miles without a six-pack. And don't head home without another.
- Ever be seen at or near a rock concert.
- Loan your knife, gun or wife to nobody.
- Let nobody from nowhere make fun of the way you talk.
- Read 'less you feel like it. An' if'n ya' do, read Southern: Lewis Grizzard, Ludlow Porch, Paul Hemphill, Robert Steed, Furman Bisher, Jerry Thompson, and Ferrol Sams.
- Go to no concerts 'less the performers play and sing country.
- Buy nothin' made outside the U.S. of A.
- Ever pass up an opportunity to praise the South and run down the North.
- Buy nothin' but white bread. Remember, a redneck wouldn't be caught dead eatin' th' likes of rye or pumpernickel. Plus English muffins and hard rolls are bad news.

THE BARE REDNECK NECESSITIES

In order that I may be of all possible assistance in effecting a smooth transition from North to South, it is imperative that certain basic items readily identifiable with the redneck lifestyle be purchased prior to departure. The mere possession of them will project the desired image upon arrival. It stands to reason that some items cannot be purchased in the North but every effort should be made to obtain them shortly after arrival in the Southland, or on the way down.

Some of the necessary items can be purchased as far north as Kentucky and Maryland. Some can be ordered from Sears and Roebuck, as well as L. L. Bean. Leave no stone unturned to complete the checklist and familiarize yourself with each item as quickly as possible.

Save the list and check off each item as it is obtained.

- Used pickup truck, with muffler and tailpipe dragging.
- One or two dogs of questionable pedigree.
- One 4 x 6 Confederate flag.
- One black cap with a yellow CAT Diesel patch.
- One belt buckle no smaller than a large pizza.
- One Army fatigue jacket with insignia removed.
- One 30.06 rifle, with scope; and one Remington Model 1100 .12 gauge shotgun. Hang both in rear window of pickup.

- Install tape player in pickup and purchase an ample supply of country music tapes, preferably by Willie Nelson, Hank Williams, Jr., Johnny Cash, "Alabama," Merle Haggard, Ricky Skaggs, David Allen Coe and Earl Thomas Conley.
- At least three Wrangler western shirts, with snaps.
- A week's supply of white socks, maybe two pair.
- An ample supply of jeans, preferably Levis.
- This is optional, but if you really want to go all out, get yourself a tattoo. The very sight of it will answer a lot of questions and open a lot of redneck doors. Two of the more popular ones are, "M-O-T-H-E-R" done in navy blue and centered in a rose pink heart on the upper left arm, and "DEATH BEFORE DISHONOR" wrapped around a dagger on the right forearm. (These can easily be obtained in either Atlantic City or Newark.)

Caution: It is strongly suggested that you refrain from having your wife or girlfriend's name or initials tattooed any place on your body. Just remember when considering same, it's a fact that a tattoo is very permanent while wives and girlfriends of rednecks ain't.

- Two or three pictures of horses and pelicans painted on black velvet. County fairs are the best source for these, and the artist will paint them while you wait. Average cost: $4.75. And buy a small light to hang over the pictures, for effect.
- Levi Garrett chewing tobacco is a must. If you don't chew and can't spit without soiling the front of your shirt and chin, by all means learn how. A redneck without Levi Garrett is like Buckingham Palace without a throne. (Buckingham Palace is in London. London is in England. England is "over yonder," somewheres.)
- At least two ashtrays mounted on the backs of plastic horses; one for the den and one for the bedroom. These can be picked up at the county fair at the same time the pictures are purchased. Just knock over a few weighted milk bottles, throw enough coins in evasive saucers or bust enough balloons with "three-for-a-dollar" darts and you've got 'em. Plan to spend about $19 per ash tray. Remember, the folks what run them concessions ain't runnin' 'em for charity.
- One Timex watch with a broken crystal. This is strong and convincing evidence that you are a working man or fight a lot, either being in your favor.
- One Zippo cigarette lighter. And get in the habit of keeping it in the watch

pocket of your Levis. Never light a female redneck's cigarette with it. That would be a dead giveaway that you are a pretender to the redneck world. Hand it to her and let her light her own cigarette. And be dang sure she returns it.

● A belt with your first name or initials burned in the back of it. This is instant status.

● One wallet-size photograph of each of your children, I mean the ones presently living with you. Rednecks always pull out the pictures of the kids when they get drunk, and rednecks do show their kids' pictures a lot. Following the photo exhibition they all gather around the bar and sing religious songs. "In the Garden" is a big favorite. If you don't know all the words, learn 'em.

- One boat paddle. Never mind that you don't own a boat. A paddle in the back of a '73 Chevy pickup speaks for itself.

- Finally, be sure there is always a copy of *National Enquirer* on the dash of the pickup. Rednecks, especially redneck women, believe the junk that's in it.

A REDNECK'S DOUBLE-WIDE IS HIS CASTLE

There's a great story still making the rounds in South Georgia concerning the separation and ultimate divorce of one Buster and his wife, Johnny Faye.

Buster and Johnny Faye had been in a state of disagreement for weeks, she accusing him of being unfaithful while he rebutted with the fact that she was not a good mother. The continuing argument peaked on a Saturday night after they had attended the weekly dance at the VFW Club in a nearby town.

"Well, I'll just tell you this!" Buster shouted as he drove to their trailer from the dance. "I have a good mind to just tell ever'body we know that I went to bed with you 'fore we ever got married! Now then, whatta' you think o' that?"

Johnny Faye bristled, and came back with, "Oh, yeah? Well, you jus' go right ahead and do that. Know what I'll do?"

"Whut?" grumbled Buster.

"I'll jus' go right behin' you and tell 'em that you won't the onliest one!"

Naturally, the divorce was forthcoming. It was finalized thirty days later and one night Buster was talking about the property settlement while shooting eight-ball in Hawkeye's Pool Room, a regular haunt for him and one of the prime factors contributing to his and Johnny Faye's divorce.

"Ever'thing went smooth as silk," he said between shots. "We jus' split ever'thing 50–50—including the double-wide."

A glance of suspicion and disbelief was cast by Hawkeye, who asked, "Aw, c'mon, Buster. How'n th' hell can you split a trailer 50–50?"

"Plumb easy, man," said Buster as he banked the nine-ball in the side pocket and chalked up to zero in on the eight. "She got th' inside an' I got th' outside."

And . . . he missed the eight-ball, straight in the corner pocket. A rarity for Buster.

It really isn't hard to spot a redneck house or trailer. Certain characteristics sort of jump out at you.

Let's take a look at the outside first.

You will find most rednecks to be three-car families; one in the front yard, usually of about 1968 vintage, with all four wheels off and sitting on four cement blocks; one in the back yard with the motor out and sitting on the ground, usually a '72 Chevrolet Impala; and the third, a '76 pickup in limited running condition, parked in front of the house under a shade tree. A dog, also in limited running condition, will be stretched out under the pickup.

In the back of the truck will be a number of crushed beer cans, a gasoline can, a five-foot section of a water hose for siphoning purposes, a coiled chain of un-determined length for towing, a dog box, a tool chest, a fishing tackle box, two fishing rods and two reels (one that works and one that don't), three blocks of wood of undetermined origin, three cans of oil and two empty oil cans, five spent shotgun shells, a spare tire (flat), a jack and three used pistons, and a boat paddle.

Inside the cab, on the dash, are three or four boxes of matches, two empty Winston cigarette packages, a beer opener, several pieces of string, sixty-seven cents in assorted coins, a State Farm Insurance calendar (opened to November although it's April), roughly 27 envelopes representing three months' overdue bills, three bolts and two nuts that fit nothing, a knife with a broken blade, a screwdriver with a broken handle, two empty boiled peanut bags, a four-year-old W-2 form, a Spearmint chewing gum wrapper, two Skoal snuff cans (one empty and the other half-filled), a throwaway letter from his congressman and a broken comb.

On the seat are two-year-old copies of *Playboy* and *Penthouse*, along with a current issue of *Parts Pups*, several cassette tapes by favorite country music artists, a publicity photograph of Dolly Parton, two cans of Vienna sausages, half a box of saltines and a Hershey bar. Also, a deck of cards, a pair of dice, two fishing lures, a

small box of fish hooks, half a box of .12 gauge shotgun shells, a fish stringer, an empty Jack Daniel's bottle, two Beef Jerkys, a Harold Robbins paperback and three hair curlers.

On the floorboard on the passenger side is a dirty T-shirt, one sneaker, three socks, two McDonald's Egg McMuffin cartons, a Hardee's coffee cup, two empty paper sacks, a pair of pliers, a crowbar, several receipts from K-Mart, two empty Levi Garrett packs, many tabs from pop-top beer cans, an equal number of Winston cigarette butts, two pieces of cuestick chalk and a county tax notice (unpaid).

Hanging in the rear window are a 30.06 deer rifle, a .12 gauge Remington Model 1100 automatic shotgun and a personalized cuestick. Also a window sticker that reads, "Member NRA."

On the back bumper are these bumper stickers: "American By Birth And Southern By The Grace Of God," "If You Must Criticize The Farmers, Don't Talk With Your Mouth Full," "Hell No, I Ain't Forgettin'!"

On the front bumper, these: "Get Your Heart In America Or Get Your Ass Out," "Southern Born And Southern Bred, And When I Die I'll Be Southern Dead," "I Found It." And a personalized plate that reads, "Joe Boy and Willie Kate."

So much for the pickup. A quick look around the yard and you'll see these trademarks:

- A tire swing hanging from a tree.
- Three or four young 'uns hanging from a tree.
- A broken TV antenna.
- A satellite dish that works.
- A washer and dryer on the front porch.
- Several chickens and a cat or two on the steps and porch.
- 12 syrup cans containing geraniums lining the walk to the front porch.
- Half-buried king-size Coke bottles between the syrup cans, just for effect.
- Half-buried whitewashed automobile tires lining the driveway. Some rotted, others needing more whitewash.
- The remains of a picket fence out by the road.
- Two bicycle tires in what was once a flower bed.
- Two mud puddles, one in the front yard and one in the back.
- A worn and rusty Honda 125 and an equally worn and rusty go-cart propped up next to the tree holding the tire swing.
- One set of bedsprings behind the utility shed.
- Another set of bedsprings in front of the utility shed.

66

● Three fishing poles leaning against the utility shed.

● A small pile of used bricks under the front steps.

● Three 55-gallon drums in the vicinity of the back door.

● One partially-finished barbeque cooker, made from a 55-gallon drum.

● One inflatable swimming pool, long ago deflated and now filled with pine needles and tadpoles. Plus a shoe and two baby diapers.

THE DIFFERENCE
BETWEEN A REDNECK AND
A GOOD OLE BOY

A redneck will stand in the door at the pool room and announce in a loud voice to one and all, "Well, it's 11:30. Time to go to the house an' eat dinner. An' I'll tell you this, too. If'n my ol' lady's got it ready, I ain't gonna' eat a damn thing; an' if'n she ain't, I'm gonna' raise hell."

A good ole boy will leave the pool room quietly, go home, and help his wife set the table and pour the tea.

A redneck will stand in front of the local Amoco station, chew his Levi Garrett, and repeatedly spit on the sidewalk.

A good ole boy will use a paper cup or step to the side of the building to unload.

A redneck walks around with a chip on his shoulder, constantly looking for an argument or a fight.

A good ole boy will do his best to avoid both, content to roll with the flow. But if pushed into a corner he will whip the daylights out of the redneck.

A redneck will ride around in his pickup, drinking beer, and throwing the empty cans out the window.

A good ole boy will throw his empty cans in the back of the pickup and drop them in a dumpster later.

A redneck spends Sunday mornings changing the oil in his pickup, drinking beer, and fishing.

A good ole boy usually can be found in church with his wife and younguns. He'll change his oil, drink his beer and go fishing Sunday afternoon.

A redneck will roll up his sleeves to his shoulders in order to display his tattoos and muscles.

Although he may have both, a good ole boy is content to leave his sleeves down and buttoned.

THE INVISIBLE SOCIETY: CLOSET REDNECKS

It's true that you can't always tell a book by its cover. Likewise, you can't always tell a redneck by the clothes he wears. And where he lives, the kind of car he drives, what his chosen profession is, or what his educational level might be provide no clues either.

In other words, what you see ain't always what you get.

I'm talkin' 'bout a special breed here, Hoss: closet rednecks. I'm talkin' 'about the fella' who's all spit an' polish. Mr. Clean during the daytime; but as soon as night falls, his colors change quicker than a chameleon. I'm talkin' 'bout the fella' who has quiche and white wine at the club for lunch and pickled pig's feet and beer at Shorty's Bar and Grill for supper.

I'm talkin' 'bout the fella' who sucks on breath mints in the office all day and pops a wad of Levi Garrett in his mouth the minute he gets home.

I'm talkin' 'bout the fella' who wears three-piece suits, oxford cloth button-down shirts, and Gucci loafers from nine to five and changes into his Levi jeans, Wrangler shirt, Tony Lama cowboy boots, and Stetson cowboy hat before headin' on down to Shorty's.

I'm talkin' 'bout the fella' who walks the straight and narrow all day and turns into a card-carrying bonafide, pop-top, put-another-quarter-in the jukebox, so's yo' mama, rebel-yellin' redneck at sundown.

Closet rednecks, that's what I'm talkin', and they are out there in droves. They're in juke joints and pool rooms from Florida to North Carolina, Georgia to Texas—and all points in between. They're doin' their thing. It's called redneckin', Hoss. And they belong to the secret society of Closet Rednecks.

I've been around juke joints all my life, and down through the years I've come to know quite a few of the closet redneck breed. In some, the trait is born and bred in them. Others acquire it through association and the desire for a partially different lifestyle, a relaxing, devil-may-care, throw-caution-to-the-wind lifestyle. No matter how they acquire the trait, closet rednecks do their thing.

Social and economic standing has no bearing whatsoever when it comes to closet rednecks. I know one in Louisiana who could buy Texas. By day, he clips coupons and watches the stock market. By night, he hits the redneck bars. Drinks beer and tomato juice.

I know another, a lawyer in Savannah, who's big in real estate. He's a closet redneck, heavy into country music. He'll drive for miles to hear a good country band. The man has more country albums than RCA. He plunks at the guitar for his own amusement and would no doubt give six condominiums if he could play like Chet Atkins.

An excellent example of a true closet redneck is my friend, Jasper D. He was born in Detroit, went to college in Michigan, and became a lawyer. He's a good one, and very successful. Jasper D. met and married a fine Georgia girl and moved south, setting up a law practice in Atlanta. The marriage lasted eight years before the divorce became final. That was five years ago. He hasn't re-married. His law practice is flourishing, and he lives in a fine townhouse in an affluent suburb.

Three years ago, the redneck bug bit Jasper, and today he is no longer Jasper. "Just call me J.D.," he tells his friends. The bug bit hard.

Before the redneck bug bit, Jasper was pretty much the prototype of a big city lawyer. You know, drive to the office in the morning, back home at night. Dinner, a little television, maybe a book. That was it. Not any more.

Jasper ("J.D.") hits the juke joints, drinks beer, knows all the songs on the jukebox at Junior's by number, and shoots pool until midnight. While his favorite restaurant before the bug bit was a fancy Atlanta restaurant, Jasper ("J.D.") can now be found most nights at suppertime at Big John's Barbeque in South Atlanta. It's easy

to tell if he's inside; just look for his
Honda Goldwing in the parking lot. It'll
be the one with the Confederate flag on
the windshield.

A few years back I was in a juke joint in
South Georgia. The place, Kitty's Korner,
was filled with rednecks, male and
female. The jukebox was going full blast,
pop-tops were popping, the pool table was
busy and the television news reporter was
receiving no attention. Kitty's was a
beehive of activity.

I hadn't been there long when I spotted
Earl, an x-ray technician. He was seated at

the end of the bar with a cold beer in front of him. His eye caught mine, and he motioned for me to join him, which I did.

"What in the world are you doing here?" I asked. "This is the last place in the world I'd expect to find you."

"Come here all the time," he said, turning up his beer.

"But you ain't no redneck, Earl, and this ain't nothin' but a redneck joint."

"Redneck? What's a redneck? All I know is that these folks in here are my kinda' folks. And the beer's cold," he said. "They work hard, they play hard, and they drink hard. An' they don't ask a man no questions. They don't give a damn who you are or where you come from. Ever'body's equal when they walk through that front door, an' that's a hell of a lot more'n I can say for some places. Buy ya' a beer?"

"Uh, yeah, thanks, Earl."

I drank the beer and left Earl talkin' to the bartender, and some girl. She was barefooted, if that means anything.

Closet rednecks. A man is likely to run into 'em most anywhere.

I have the feeling that sooner or later the real rednecks, the ones who work at it full time, are going to reach the point where they question closet rednecks invading their territory. I wouldn't be at all surprised if they didn't come up with some sort of entrance exam that a closet redneck had to take before he would be allowed to enter the real redneck world, even on a part-time basis. In view of this, I have devised such an exam that the rednecks might consider. Just 10 questions:

1. Have you ever swallowed lard?
2. Do you now, or have you ever owned a motorcycle?
3. Can you bench press a VW?
4. Do you bathe more than twice a week?
5. How many pairs of boots do you own?
6. Which do you carry, a knife or a pistol?
7. Do you know Willie Nelson's middle name?
8. Have you ever totaled a pickup?
9. How many times you been arrested for fightin'?
10. Can you read and rite? How good?

One prime example of a closet redneck is the case of a Birmingham, Alabama, doctor. His wife, Sarah Jane, related to me just how the transformation from M.D. by day to redneck by night takes place.

"You wouldn't believe he's the same man," Sarah Jane says. "All day long he's in his well-appointed and fashionable office seeing patients as the highly respectable medical specialist that he is. He's decked out in his starched-just-right blue button-down oxford shirt, his ultra-conservative tie, banker's gray trousers and black Florsheim tassel loafers. His styled hair is perfectly groomed and he wears just enough Polo cologne to be interesting. His white medical coat is starched to perfection, and his stethoscope is ever-present in his pocket or dangling around his neck. The nine-to-five picture is that of professionalism personified. And his immaculately manicured nails grip the steering wheel of his equally immaculately manicured Mercedes when he drives back and forth to the hospital to see patients and perform surgery."

But, according to Sarah Jane, the good doctor comes out of the closet the minute he arrives at their suburban mansion home from his office. "You wouldn't know he was the same man," she says.

So. What happens to the good doctor when the sun goes down? This is what his wife says:

"The first thing he does is shed his working clothes. Off come the shirt, tie, conservative trousers and spit-shined shoes. Within minutes, he emerges from the bedroom decked in his old and faded

jeans, cowboy boots, denim shirt, a
Charlie Daniels hat and chewing Levi Garrett tobacco. He heads straight for the
back yard and walks right on by the Mercedes like it wasn't there and jumps into
his prized vehicle, a 1968 Chevy pickup
with oversize tires. He then inserts a
Willie Nelson tape and blasts off in a
cloud of dust. Where does he go? He just
rides and rides, chewing tobacco, spitting
and listening to Willie Nelson. Most of the
time he's gone for over an hour, and he's
happy as a lark when he returns and
brakes to a stop behind the Mercedes.
What he's done is make the transformation—from surgeon to redneck.

According to Sarah Jane, the good doctor's transformation doesn't end when he
parks his pickup. There's more to come
after dinner (supper).

"Most nights he retires to the den after
dinner for about an hour. He gets on the
telephone and calls old friends back
home, in Arkansas. And I'll tell you, you
would never know it was the same man
that spent the day engaged in his profession as a doctor. The minute he gets on
that telephone to Arkansas his entire manner of talking and conversing changes
completely. 'How are you?' suddenly becomes 'How y'all doin'?' and 'How are
your parents getting along?' changes to

'How's y'r mommerem?' Such things as 'Shoot I reckon!' 'Ya' better bleeve it! and I ain't never', emanate from the den. And when he's finished, does he say, 'Well, you'll have to excuse me, Roger, but I really must go?' Not on your life. It's 'See ya' 'round, Hoss. I gotta' bring this to a screechin' halt.' So you see, I really have two husbands, a surgeon by day and a redneck by night."

After hearing Sarah Jane's story, I am more convinced than ever that there is a definite need for a Closet Redneck Society, a club if you will, that would welcome such men with open arms; a club that would afford such professionals the opportunity to vent their true feelings after a long, hard day at the office. Indeed, a place where they can "let it all hang out."

DEER HUNTING

Hunting is one of a redneck's favorite activities. But, as with all things, there's a right way to do it.

♦ ♦ ♦ ♦ ♦

Two New Jersey Americans went deer hunting for the first time near Willacoochee. One killed a big buck just after daylight and they began dragging it by the tail to the pickup truck more than a mile away.

A Willacoochee native saw them as they struggled past his stand, almost out of breath. They were within sight of the pickup, about 300 yards away.

"I b'leeve you boys'd have a easier time of it draggin' that buck by the horns," he told them.

They heeded his suggestion, walked to the deer's head, took a firm grip on his 12-point rack and began dragging. After thirty minutes they stopped to catch their breath.

"That fellow was right," one said. "Sure is a heck of a lot easier to pull this deer by the horns than by the tail, ain't it?"

"Yeah," said the other, "but have you noticed how far away from the truck we're getting?"

◆ ◆ ◆ ◆ ◆

Now I'm not saying that the following is the *right* way to do it, but show me a hunter who won't admit to having at least one deer huntin' experience like it, and I'll show you one who makes me leery of his honesty.

"DIARY OF A DEER HUNTER"

- 1:00 A.M.: SATURDAY. Alarm clock rings.
- 2:00 A.M.: Hunting partners arrive and drag you out of bed.
- 2:30 A.M.: Throw everything in pickup except kitchen sink.
- 3:00 A.M.: Leave for the deep woods.
- 3:15 A.M.: Drive back home to pick up gun.

- 3:30 A.M.: Drive like crazy to get to woods before daylight.
- 4:00 A.M.: Set up camp . . . forgot stupid tent.
- 4:30 A.M.: Head into woods, climb tree, get in stand.
- 5:15 A.M.: Take first shot of antifreeze.
- 5:20 A.M.: Attempt to light cigarette with wet match.
- 5:31 A.M.: Walk back to pickup to use cigarette lighter.
- 6:00 A.M.: Back in tree—second shot of antifreeze.
- 6:05 A.M.: Spot eight deer while lighting second cigarette from butt of first cigarette.
- 6:06 A.M.: Drop cigarette, take aim through scope and squeeze trigger.
- 6:06:08: "CLICK"
- 6:07 A.M.: Load gun while watching eight deer disappear over hill.
- 8:00 A.M.: Head back to camp for breakfast.
- 9:00 A.M.: Still looking for camp. Recognize tree you climbed out of an hour earlier.
- 9:12 A.M.: Try again to light cigarette with wet match.
- 9:14 A.M.: Rub two sticks together in vain attempt to start fire. Re-

alize why you never advanced beyond rank of Tenderfoot in Boy Scouts.

- 10:00 A.M.: Face the fact that you don't know where you are.

- NOON: FIRE GUN REPEATEDLY FOR HELP. EAT WILD BERRIES FOR LUNCH.

- 12:15 P.M.: The eight deer come back . . . CLICK . . . All out of bullets.
- 12:20 P.M.: Strange feeling in stomach.
- 12:30 P.M.: Realize you ate poison berries for lunch.
- 12:45 P.M.: RESCUED.
- 12:55 P.M.: Rushed to hospital to have stomach pumped out.
- 3:00 P.M.: Arrive back in camp.
- 3:30 P.M.: Leave camp and walk back to deer stand.
- 4:00 P.M.: Walk back to camp for bullets.
- 4:01 P.M.: Load gun and leave camp again.
- 5:00 P.M.: Empty gun on squirrel that's been bugging you.
- 6:00 P.M.: Arrive back at camp . . . see deer grazing in camp.
- 6:01 P.M.: Load gun.
- 6:01:13: FIRE GUN.

- 6:02 P.M.: ONE DEAD PICKUP TRUCK.
- 6:05 P.M.: Hunting partner returns to camp dragging deer with 13-point rack you missed at 6:02 P.M.
- 6:06 P.M.: Suppress strong desire to shoot hunting partner.
- 6:07 P.M.: Stumble over hunting partner's deer and fall into campfire.
- 6:15 P.M.: Take pickup—leave hunting partner and his deer in woods.
- 6:25 P.M.: Radiator boils over due to hole shot in motor block.

- 6:26 P.M.: Start walking.
- 6:30 P.M.: Trip over stump, stumble and fall. Drop gun in mud. Retrieve it and keep walking.
- 6:35 P.M.: Meet bear head-on.
- 6:35:01: Aim and fire at bear. Blow up gun barrel that's plugged with mud.
- 6:35:04: MESSED UP PANTS.
- 6:35:08: Cast gun down and climb up nearby tree.
- 9:05 P.M.: Bear departs. Climb down out of tree. Retrieve gun and wrap around tree. Start walking.
- MIDNIGHT: Home at last. Light cigarette with dry match and pour third shot (double) of antifreeze.
- 1:00 P.M.: SUNDAY. Watch football on TV while slowly tearing hunting license in little pieces.

HOW CAN YANKEES BLEND IN WITH SOUTHERN LIVING?

This is an open letter to those thundering herds of carpetbaggers who are seriously considering migrating south into Georgia, Texas and other Southern states.

It ain't easy to just pull up stakes and move off to a new region of the country and blend in immediately. Just ask any good ol' Southern boy forced to move north to Chicago, Detroit, Newark or New York City.

But if you are bound and determined to make the move to Dixie, here are some tips on how a Yankee can ease into the redneck life in the South with minimal difficulty. (Note: These tips apply to all states south of the Mason-Dixon line except Florida, which is really nothing

more than one giant rest home for New York City and New Jersey folks.)

O.K., here we go.

● Sell your BMW. It screams "Yankee" at every turn.

● Buy a pickup truck, preferably 1973–78 vintage.

● Add a gun rack across the rear window of the cab and replace the conventional tires with big 'uns.

● Install a tape player and buy two tapes to start with, "Moe and Joe Bandy" and "Waylon and Willie and the Boys."

- Weld a trailer hitch to the back bumper and place a hound dog of dubious lineage in the back. Name him "Scrap Iron."
- Go to the nearest five and ten, buy a pair of those big fuzzy dice and hang them from the rear view mirror. If you have a pair of baby shoes and the tassel from your graduation cap, hang them, too.

These things accomplished, you will have taken a giant step in the direction toward gaining provisional status as a good ole boy in the South. But disregard above if it is your intention to re-locate in Atlanta. It ain't a Southern city no more, what with the Yankee money taking over and all. Shoot! In Atlanta now a fellow has to go days on end without hearing a Southern accent, and English itself is struggling to remain afloat.

Be that as it may, here's a word about dress for those staying on Interstate 75 and ignoring Atlanta for points further South:

- Learn to dress casually. Divest yourself of those tight-fitting designer suits and lizard-skin Italian shoes that seem to be so popular with certain New

Yorkers and short, swarthy, just-arrived South American Latins.

● Ideally, you should have two wardrobes of jeans. The dirt-slicked, worn-out-at-the-knees kind (with a circular imprint of a snuff can on the rear pocket) will suffice for everyday wear. But you'll need a couple of faded, but clean pairs with razor-sharp creases down the front for Sundays and special occasions. You know, like the ones them Grand Ole Opry stars wear with their tuxedo coats at the Country Music Awards show on television. But no belt. Don't wear no belt. That ain't macho.

● And whatever you do, don't be seen in public in a pair of designer jeans. Good ole boys just flat don't wear Calvin Kleins in Dixie—dead or alive. But if you've got some, don't throw 'em away. Save 'em for when you go back to New York on vacation.

● Forget the blue oxford cloth button-down preppy dress shirts like you and your old lady wear. T-shirts with gross sayings on them will serve the purpose just fine. Be sure and get at least one with *Harley Davidson* on it.

● For special occasions and Sundays, a denim work shirt and leather jacket that looks like it was made from your grand-

mother's old oilcloth tablecloth is as near as a good ole boy comes to haute couture.

• Depending on your job, you may have to do something with your hair. Office workers, lawyers and assorted other professionals can get by with hair carefully groomed and frozen into place with hair spray. But . . . if your plan is to work in construction, road building, sheetrock hanging, becoming a country music singer or hitting the unemployment line upon arrival, you dang well better let it grow long.

• Pick up a cheap, used guitar and learn a couple of songs before you head south. Country songs are strongly suggested, something like "Release Me," and maybe "Born to Lose."

● Forget that skeet shooting and archery ever existed. These Yankee luxuries are practiced in the deep south only on South Carolina and south Georgia plantations owned by the ultimate carpetbaggers— David Rockefeller, William F. Buckley and John Hay Whitney. Forget them and find yourself a local coon hunting club. If there's not one around the area where you locate, there's always the weekly Lion's Club turkey shoot.

● Right off, start hanging around the neighborhood Amoco station in the evening and the pool room in the daytime. It's good practice for standing around outside a church on Wednesday night talkin' huntin' and fishin' with the other boys while the wife and the young 'uns are inside at prayer meeting.

● Learn to spit a lot. Rednecks and good ole boys are big spitters.

● Pay your child support on time.

● Understand there are some things you will be expected to get excited about: Fishing, hunting, motorcycles, pickup trucks, dogs, 18-wheelers, the Grand Ole Opry, Levi Garrett chewing tobacco, wrestling, gospel music, and county fairs.

- Learn to talk with a kitchen match in your mouth.
- Leave your list of vintage wines in Yankeeland. Beer's the name of the game in Dixie.

Finally, your name.

- If your name happens to be Maurice or Bruce, you'll never make it in redneck country unless you make the switch to initials. Start now calling yourself "M.C." or "J.D."
- Of course, you could go all the way and have your name legally changed to Bubba, the ultimate redneck status symbol. It will open almost as many doors for you as, well, Robert E. Lee.
- Females can't go wrong by assuming double names. Ethel, Penelope, Gertrude or Sheila won't get it. Such names as Robbie Nell, Willie Kate, Martha Ann, Johnnie Faye, Gloria Jean, Kathy Sue and Mattie Bee guarantee almost immediate acceptance without explanation.

If you can bring yourself to make these suggested adjustments you are well on your way to making the move to redneck country.

Bo Whaley has won twenty-one awards as a
columnist for the Dublin, Georgia, *Courier
Herald*. He speaks to more than 200 au-
diences each year, hosts a morning radio talk
show, is the author of *Rednecks and Other
Bonafide Americans*, *The Official Redneck
Handbook*, and *How to Love Yankees with a
Clear Conscience*, "and loafs a lot."